TABLE OF CONTENTS

INTRODUCTION 1

CHAPTER ONE: MANAGING CIRCUMSTANCES IN A PHOBIA-FILLED WORLD 2

CHAPTER TWO: UNDERSTANDING SOCIAL PHOBIA 16

CHAPTER THREE: WHAT YOU NEED TO KNOW ABOUT AGORAPHOBIA.................................21

CHAPTER FOUR: KNOWING NOSOPHOBIA WITH THE RIGHT SUPPORT.................................25

CHAPTER FIVE: ILLNESS ANXIETY DISORDER 29

CHAPTER SIX: DEALING WITH MYSOPHOBIA IN A SPECIAL WAY 33

CHAPTER SEVEN: TIMELY HANDLING OF ACROPHOBIA 37

CHAPTER EIGHT: OVERCOMING AEROPHOBIA 41

CHAPTER NINE: PRACTICALLY DEALING WITH ASTRAPHOBIA 45

CHAPTER TEN : TRUE PICTURE OF TRYPANOPHOBIA FOR GOOD MEDICAL BENEFITS.........................47

CHAPTER ELEVEN: TRUTH ABOUT XENOPHOBIA 50

CHAPTER TWELVE: HIDDEN FACTORS ABOUT DEATH PHOBIA 56

CHAPTER THIRTEEN: ANIMAL PHOBIA TREATMENT 58

CONCLUSION 69

INTRODUCTION

I'm terrified! I'm scared because of a negative pandemic experience I had recently. It's not amusing. When I come across terrorists, I'm always terrified. I can't even attempt to remember what happened when I narrowly avoided dying during a shooting. You can continue by sharing your phobia-related experiences with people all over the globe. As long as there have been humans, there have been phobias. Phobias are a part of human nature by default. No matter how self-assured you are, phobias will inevitably strike at some time in your life.

You might feel the most helpless or afraid individual on Earth when that happens. The ideal course of action, if you could have your way, would be to get rid of your phobia. The good news is that as long as you can understand and manage your phobia, there won't be much to fret about.

People have had phobias for as long as there have been people.Phobias are a natural component of human nature. No matter how confident you are as a person, it is inevitable that you will experience phobias at some point. When that occurs, you might feel the most helpless or afraid person on Earth. It's fascinating to note that you won't have much to worry about if you can comprehend and control your phobia.

An intense and irrational dread of a particular thing, circumstance, or activity that presents little to no real risk is known as a phobia. It is associated with a particular trigger, like an animal, a needle, or an elevator. A specific phobia is a type of anxiety disorder that causes individuals to experience excessive levels of fear in comparison to the actual threat that the phobia's trigger presents. In exceptional situations, such as during a plane crash, traveling by plane, for example, can be risky, but most people admit that such an event is unlikely and that flying is usually secure. For someone with a specific fear of flying, getting on an airplane represents a possibly fatal risk.

There are many causes of anxiety disorders like phobias, but experts believe a combination of genetic and environmental variables is to blame. For example, children who experience stress during development and have a family background of anxiety disorders are more likely to experience certain phobias. People who develop a specific phobia display specific symptoms, such as experiencing intense worry when exposed to the phobia's trigger and going out of their way to avoid it.

Numerous global events have the potential to trigger phobias because they can be stressful experiences that have an ever-lasting effect on people's psyches. Several instances include:

War and terrorism: People who experience or witness acts of war or terrorism may develop a phobia of crowds, loud noises, or certain types of vehicles such as planes or buses.

War and terrorism can cause phobia through various ways. Here are a few examples:

Direct exposure to violence: People who witness or experience violence directly during a war or terrorist attack may develop phobias related to the triggers that caused the trauma. For example, someone who survived a bombing may develop a phobia of loud noises or crowded places.

Indirect exposure to violence: People who are not directly involved in a war or terrorist attack but are exposed to images or stories of the violence through the media or conversations with others may also develop phobias. For example, seeing images of bombings or hearing stories of terrorist attacks may lead to a phobia of crowded public spaces.

Generalized anxiety: War and terrorism can create a sense of uncertainty and fear in society as a whole, leading to generalized anxiety and a heightened state of alertness. This can lead to phobias related to safety and security.

Post-Traumatic Stress Disorder (PTSD): PTSD is a mental health condition that can develop after exposure to a traumatic event. People with PTSD may experience intrusive thoughts, flashbacks, and nightmares related to the trauma, which can lead to phobias and other anxiety disorders.

Overall, war and terrorism can cause phobias by creating a sense of fear, uncertainty, and trauma in individuals and society as a whole. It is important to seek professional help if you or someone you know is struggling with a phobia or any other mental health issue related to these events.

Ways to handle war and Terrorism phobia

Dealing with war and terrorism phobia can be challenging, but there are ways to manage and reduce its impact on daily life. Here are some strategies that may help:

Seek professional help: If you are experiencing significant anxiety, fear, or distress related to war and terrorism, it may be helpful to seek the support of a mental health professional. A therapist can provide you with tools and strategies to manage your symptoms, such as cognitive-behavioral therapy (CBT), exposure therapy, and relaxation techniques.

Stay informed, but limit media exposure: It is important to stay informed about current events, but it can be overwhelming to consume constant news coverage of war and terrorism. Consider setting limits on your media exposure and focusing on reliable sources of information.

Connect with others: Talking with friends, family, or a support group can be helpful in reducing feelings of isolation and anxiety. It can also provide a sense of community and support.

Practice self-care: Taking care of yourself physically and emotionally can help reduce anxiety and stress related to war and terrorism. Engage in activities that promote relaxation and mindfulness, such as meditation, yoga, or deep breathing exercises.

Take action: Engaging in activism or volunteer work related to causes that you care about can help you feel empowered and make a positive impact in your community.

Remember, managing war and terrorism phobia is a process, and it may take time to find strategies that work best for you. It is essential to be patient and kind to yourself during this process.

Natural disasters: Earthquakes, floods, hurricanes, and other natural disasters can cause people to develop a phobia of similar events or the elements that cause them.

Natural disasters can cause phobia in several ways. Firstly, the experience of being in a natural disaster, such as a hurricane, earthquake, or tornado, can be extremely traumatic. This traumatic experience can create an association between the natural disaster and fear, leading to the development of a phobia.

Second, certain phobias connected to a particular natural disaster may emerge as a result of the disaster. For instance, someone who experiences a flood might acquire a fear of water, whereas someone who encounters a tornado might do the same. You might also consider phobias connected to recent disasters such as earthquakes that have wreaked havoc in some nations. They had been extremely devastating occurrences that had seriously damaged houses, communities, and infrastructure. They had also resulted in harm and fatalities, which were very upsetting for those impacted.

If you were personally affected by the earthquake, it's important to prioritize your safety and seek help if you need it. You can contact emergency services, such as ambulance or rescue teams, if you or someone else requires immediate medical attention. You can also reach out to local authorities or community organizations for support with shelter, food, and other basic needs.

In addition, earthquakes can be very traumatic events that can cause emotional distress and anxiety. If you are experiencing symptoms of anxiety or distress, it's important to seek support from a mental health professional. They can help you to cope with the effects of the earthquake and manage any ongoing stress or anxiety.

It's also important to stay informed about the situation and follow any guidance from local authorities. This can help to keep you and your loved ones safe during and after the earthquake.

Finally, natural disasters can also lead to the development of generalized anxiety disorder (GAD). GAD is a type of anxiety disorder characterized by excessive worry and anxiety about a range of events or activities. Natural disasters can be a trigger for GAD, leading to ongoing anxiety and fear about future disasters.

It's important to note that not everyone who experiences a natural disaster will develop a phobia or anxiety disorder. However, for those who do, it can have a significant impact on their quality of life and mental health. Seeking support from a mental health professional can be helpful in managing the effects of natural disasters on mental health.

Pandemics: The COVID-19 pandemic has led to an increase in phobias related to germs, public places, and travel.

Covid-19, also known as the coronavirus, can cause phobia in a number of ways. Here are some possible ways:

Fear of infection: The most obvious way Covid-19 can cause phobia is by triggering a fear of infection. People may become so scared of catching the virus that they avoid leaving their homes or interacting with others, even after the pandemic subsides. This can lead to a phobia of germs, known as mysophobia or germophobia.

Trauma from illness: For people who have had Covid-19 or know someone who has, the experience can be traumatic. The symptoms of the virus can be severe and sometimes require hospitalization. This traumatic experience can lead to a phobia of illness, also known as nosophobia.

Fear of death: Covid-19 has caused many deaths worldwide, and the fear of dying from the virus can lead to a phobia of death, known as thanatophobia. People who have lost loved ones to the virus may be particularly susceptible to this type of phobia.

Anxiety and uncertainty: The pandemic has caused a great deal of anxiety and uncertainty for many people. The constantly changing information and recommendations from health officials can be overwhelming, leading to a phobia of uncertainty, known as decidophobia.

Social phobia: The pandemic has also changed the way people interact with each other, with many people choosing to social distance or avoid large gatherings. This can lead to a phobia of social situations, known as social anxiety disorder.

It's important to note that not everyone who experiences fear or anxiety related to Covid-19 will develop a phobia. However, for those who do, therapy and other forms of treatment can be effective in managing and overcoming their phobia.

Mass shootings: People who have been directly or indirectly impacted by mass shootings may develop a phobia of crowded public spaces or certain types of events.

Mass shootings can create phobia, which is an intense and irrational fear, in several ways:

Media coverage: Mass shootings often receive extensive media coverage, with images and videos of the event being replayed repeatedly on television and social media. This can lead to a sense of constant exposure to the traumatic event, which can trigger anxiety and fear in people who were not directly affected by the shooting.

Personal connection: People who have a personal connection to a mass shooting, such as having a family member or friend who was a victim, may develop a phobia as a result of the trauma they experienced. They may begin to fear that a similar event could happen again, either to them or to someone they care about.

Vicarious trauma: Even people who do not have a personal connection to a mass shooting can experience vicarious trauma, which is a form of trauma that occurs when someone witnesses or hears about a traumatic event happening to others. This can lead to symptoms of anxiety, depression, and PTSD, which can contribute to the development of a phobia.

Perception of safety: Mass shootings can also create a general sense of insecurity and a perception that public places are no longer safe. This can lead people to avoid certain places or activities out of fear, which can further reinforce their phobia.

Overall, mass shootings can create a sense of fear and uncertainty that can lead to the development of a phobia, especially in people who are already prone to anxiety or trauma. It's important to seek support and treatment if you are experiencing symptoms of a phobia related to mass shootings or any other traumatic event.

Sexual assault or violence: Survivors of sexual assault or violence may develop a phobia of certain situations or people that remind them of their trauma.

Sexual assault is a traumatic event that can have lasting effects on a person's mental health. One way that sexual assault can lead to phobia is through the development of post-traumatic stress disorder (PTSD). PTSD is a mental health condition that can develop after a person experiences or witnesses a traumatic event, such as sexual assault.

People with PTSD may experience intrusive thoughts or memories of the traumatic event, nightmares, and intense emotional reactions to triggers that remind them of the trauma. They may also try to avoid anything that reminds them of the trauma, including people, places, or situations that are associated with the assault.

In some cases, this avoidance can become so extreme that it develops into a phobia. For example, a person who was sexually assaulted in a park may develop a phobia of parks or outdoor spaces. This phobia can be so intense that the person avoids going outside altogether, which can significantly impact their quality of life.Sexual assault can also lead to other types of phobias, such as a fear of intimacy or a fear of being vulnerable. These phobias can develop as a result of the loss of control that often accompanies sexual assault, and they can make it difficult for a person to form intimate relationships or trust others.

Overall, sexual assault can have a profound impact on a person's mental health and well-being, and it is important for survivors to seek professional help to address any symptoms or challenges they may be experiencing.

Airplane crashes: People who have experienced or witnessed an airplane crash may develop a phobia of flying or being in enclosed spaces.

How airplane crashes cause phobia

Airplane crashes can cause phobia or fear of flying, also known as aviophobia, for several reasons:

Media Coverage: Whenever there is a plane crash, it is usually covered extensively by the media. This media coverage can be traumatic for people who have a fear of flying and may reinforce their belief that flying is dangerous.

Personal Experience: People who have experienced a close call or a turbulent flight may develop a fear of flying. A traumatic experience like this can leave a lasting impression, and the fear can linger long after the flight has ended.

Loss of Control: Some people may develop a fear of flying because they feel that they have no control over the situation. When you are on a plane, you are completely at the mercy of the pilot and the crew. This loss of control can be unnerving for some people.

Fear of Heights: Some people may have a fear of heights, and flying on a plane can trigger this fear. Even though the plane is safe and secure, the thought of being thousands of feet in the air can be terrifying for some.

Anxiety and Panic Attacks: Flying can be stressful, and people who are prone to anxiety or panic attacks may find flying to be overwhelming. The anticipation of the flight, the crowds, the security checks, and the unfamiliar environment can all contribute to anxiety and panic attacks.

In summary, airplane crashes can cause phobia by triggering traumatic memories, creating a sense of helplessness, exacerbating fear of heights, and inducing anxiety and panic attacks.

It's important to note that not everyone who experiences these events will develop a phobia, and that phobias can also develop from more everyday experiences. However, traumatic events can be a triggering factor for many people.. Right now, it would be best to list the various phobias that have impacted people throughout history and consider what we can learn from them about how to handle similar circumstances.

Social phobia

Social phobia, also known as social anxiety disorder, is a type of anxiety disorder characterized by excessive fear, self-consciousness, and anxiety in social situations. People with social phobia may fear being humiliated, embarrassed, or judged negatively by others, even in situations that are not inherently threatening.

Social phobia has been recognized as a mental health condition for centuries, although it has been known by different names throughout history.

In the late 1800s, German psychiatrist Emil Kraepelin first described "psychic impotence," which he believed to be a form of anxiety related to social situations.

Kraepelin's work was followed by that of Sigmund Freud, who recognized social phobia as a form of anxiety disorder.

However, it was not until the 1960s that social phobia was formally recognized as a distinct mental health condition. In 1964, psychiatrist Isaac Marks coined the term "social phobia" to describe a condition characterized by intense fear of social situations. Marks' work helped to establish social phobia as a distinct anxiety disorder, and it was included in the Diagnostic and Statistical Manual of Mental Disorders (DSM) in 1980.

Since then, research has continued to deepen our understanding of social phobia and its causes, as well as to develop effective treatments for the condition. Today, social phobia is recognized as a common and treatable mental health condition that affects millions of people worldwide.

Symptoms of social phobia can include sweating, trembling, blushing, difficulty speaking, and avoidance of social situations. The fear and avoidance can lead to significant impairment in daily functioning, including difficulties in forming and maintaining relationships, performing at work or school, and participating in social activities.

While there is no definitive evidence of an increasing rise in social phobia, there is some evidence to suggest that the prevalence of the condition may be increasing.

One study published in the Journal of Anxiety Disorders in 2017 found that the prevalence of social anxiety disorder had increased significantly in recent years, particularly among adolescents and young adults. The study analyzed data from several large-scale surveys conducted over the past two decades and found that the prevalence of social anxiety disorder had increased from 7.9% in the early 2000s to 12.1% in the mid-2010s.

There are several potential explanations for this increase in social phobia. One possibility is that the rise of social media and other forms of digital communication may be contributing to increased feelings of social isolation and anxiety. Another possibility is that changes in societal expectations and pressures, such as increased emphasis on achievement and success, may be contributing to increased anxiety and social phobia.

However, it is also important to note that changes in diagnostic criteria and increased awareness of social phobia may also be contributing to the apparent increase in prevalence. It is difficult to draw definitive conclusions about the reasons behind any potential rise in social phobia, and more research is needed to better understand this complex condition.

Effects of social phobia

Social phobia can have significant negative effects on an individual's life, including:

Impaired social functioning: Social phobia can significantly impair an individual's ability to function in social situations. They may avoid social situations altogether or endure them with intense fear and discomfort, which can affect their ability to make friends, maintain relationships, and pursue their goals.

Physical symptoms: Social phobia can cause physical symptoms such as sweating, shaking, blushing, and rapid heartbeat. These symptoms can be embarrassing and may further contribute to the individual's fear of social situations.

Depression and other mental health problems: Social phobia is often comorbid with other mental health conditions, such as depression and substance abuse. The fear and isolation associated with social phobia can also contribute to low self-esteem and a negative self-image.

Occupational and educational difficulties: Social phobia can interfere with an individual's ability to perform in educational and occupational settings, particularly those that require public speaking, group work, or frequent interaction with others.

Reduced quality of life: Social phobia can significantly reduce an individual's overall quality of life, leading to feelings of loneliness, isolation, and dissatisfaction with life.

Treatment for social phobia can include cognitive-behavioral therapy, medication, or a combination of both. Cognitive-behavioral therapy involves identifying and challenging negative thoughts and beliefs related to social situations, and gradually exposing oneself to feared situations in a controlled and supportive environment. Medications such as selective serotonin reuptake inhibitors (SSRIs) can also be effective in reducing symptoms of social phobia.

CHAPTER THREE: WHAT YOU NEED TO KNOW ABOUT AGORAPHOBIA

Agoraphobia is a type of anxiety disorder characterized by a fear of situations or places where

might be difficult or help might not be available in the event of an unexpected panic attack or other distressing symptoms. People with agoraphobia often avoid crowded places, public transportation, shopping centers, and other situations that may trigger anxiety or panic.

Agoraphobia can be quite disabling and can interfere with a person's ability to carry out daily activities, such as going to work or school, socializing with friends and family, or running errands. It can also lead to depression, substance abuse, and other mental health issues.

Treatment for agoraphobia may involve a combination of medications and therapy, including cognitive-behavioral therapy (CBT), exposure therapy, and other forms of psychotherapy. With proper treatment, many people with agoraphobia can learn to manage their symptoms and live full, productive lives.

Events that leads to agrophobia

Agoraphobia can be caused by a combination of genetic, environmental, and psychological factors. Some possible events or experiences that may lead to the development of agoraphobia include:

Trauma: Experiencing a traumatic event, such as a car accident or assault, can trigger anxiety and panic attacks, which may eventually lead to agoraphobia.

Panic disorder: People with panic disorder, which is characterized by recurrent and unexpected panic attacks, may develop agoraphobia as a way to avoid situations that may trigger their symptoms.

Chronic illness: People with chronic illnesses, such as heart disease or chronic pain, may develop agoraphobia as a result of their fear of experiencing a medical emergency in a public place.

Substance abuse: Substance abuse can lead to anxiety and panic attacks, which may eventually lead to agoraphobia.

Genetics: There may be a genetic component to agoraphobia, as it tends to run in families.

Environmental factors: Living in a high-stress environment, such as a high-crime neighborhood, can increase the risk of developing agoraphobia.

It's important to note that not everyone who experiences these events or factors will develop agoraphobia, and some people may develop agoraphobia without any obvious trigger. It's also possible for agoraphobia to develop gradually over time, without any specific triggering event.

Treatment for agrophobia

Treatment for agoraphobia typically involves a combination of medication and psychotherapy, including the following:

Cognitive-behavioral therapy (CBT): CBT is a type of talk therapy that can be effective in treating agoraphobia. It involves identifying negative or irrational thought patterns that contribute to anxiety and replacing them with more positive and rational ones. CBT may also involve exposure therapy, which involves gradually exposing the person to situations that trigger their anxiety, in a controlled and safe manner, until they become desensitized to them.

Medication: Antidepressants and anti-anxiety medications can be helpful in treating agoraphobia, especially when used in conjunction with psychotherapy. These medications can help alleviate symptoms of anxiety, panic, and depression.

Relaxation techniques: Learning relaxation techniques, such as deep breathing, meditation, and progressive muscle relaxation, can be helpful in managing symptoms of anxiety and panic.

Lifestyle changes: Making lifestyle changes, such as getting regular exercise, getting enough sleep, and avoiding alcohol and caffeine, can help reduce symptoms of anxiety and improve overall mental health.

It's important to seek treatment as soon as possible if you think you may have agoraphobia, as this condition can be very debilitating and can interfere with your ability to live a full and productive life. With proper treatment, however, many people with agoraphobia are able to manage their symptoms and live a fulfilling life.

CHAPTER FOUR: KNOWING NOSOPHOBIA WITH THE RIGHT SUPPORT

Nosophobia is a type of anxiety disorder that is characterized by an excessive fear of disease or illness. It is also sometimes referred to as hypochondriasis, health anxiety or illness anxiety disorder.

People with nosophobia are often preoccupied with the idea that they have or will develop a serious illness or disease, even when there is little or no evidence to support such a belief. They may constantly check their bodies for signs of illness, such as lumps or bumps, or they may become fixated on a particular symptom or sensation, such as a headache or chest pain.

This excessive worry and preoccupation with illness can lead to significant distress and impairment in daily functioning. People with nosophobia may avoid certain activities or situations that they perceive as increasing their risk of getting sick. They may also seek out multiple medical opinions and tests, even when there is no clear medical indication for doing so.

Treatment for nosophobia typically involves a combination of cognitive-behavioral therapy (CBT), medication, and self-help techniques such as relaxation training and stress management. The goal of treatment is to help individuals learn to manage their anxiety and fear of illness, and to develop more realistic and rational beliefs about their health.

History about Nosophobia

Nosophobia is a term used to describe an extreme and irrational fear of contracting or developing a disease. The term comes from the Greek word "noso," meaning disease, and "phobia," meaning fear. The fear of illness has been a part of human experience for thousands of years and has been documented in various cultures throughout history.

In ancient times, many cultures believed that illnesses were caused by evil spirits or gods punishing individuals for their sins. As a result, people would often engage in rituals or make offerings to the gods in order to ward off illness or appease them.

During the Middle Ages, when pandemics like the Black Death swept through Europe, fear of illness reached new heights. Many people believed that the disease was caused by "miasma," or bad air, and that it was spread by contact with infected individuals. This led to widespread paranoia and the persecution of individuals believed to be carriers of the disease, such as Jews and lepers.

In the 19th and 20th centuries, advances in medical science led to a better understanding of the causes of disease and the development of vaccines and treatments for many illnesses. However, the fear of illness continued to persist, particularly during times of epidemic or pandemic outbreaks, such as the Spanish Flu of 1918-1919 and the current COVID-19 pandemic.

Today, nosophobia remains a common fear, and many individuals may experience anxiety or distress related to the possibility of contracting a serious illness.

However, with the availability of medical treatments and preventative measures such as vaccines, the risk of many illnesses can be greatly reduced, and individuals who experience nosophobia can seek treatment to manage their fears.

Help for people suffering from Nosophobia

If you are experiencing nosophobia, there are several steps you can take to manage your fears and anxiety:

Seek support: It's important to talk to someone you trust about your fears and concerns. This could be a friend, family member, or a mental health professional who can help you develop coping strategies.

Educate yourself: Learning more about the illness you fear can help you gain a better understanding of the risks involved and how to minimize them. However, it's important to rely on reputable sources of information and avoid getting overwhelmed by excessive exposure to news or social media coverage.

Practice good hygiene: Practicing good hygiene, such as washing your hands regularly and covering your mouth when coughing or sneezing, can help reduce the risk of contracting or spreading illnesses.

Seek professional help: If your fear of illness is interfering with your daily life and causing significant distress, consider seeking help from a mental health professional. Cognitive-behavioral therapy (CBT) and exposure therapy can be effective treatments for nosophobia.

Consider medication: In some cases, medication such as anti-anxiety or antidepressant medications may be prescribed to help manage symptoms.

Remember, nosophobia is a common fear, and you are not alone. With the right support and treatment, it's possible to manage your fears and live a fulfilling life.

CHAPTER FIVE: ILLNESS ANXIETY DISORDER

Illness anxiety disorder (IAD), previously known as hypochondriasis, is a condition characterized by excessive preoccupation or worry about having a serious illness despite the absence of any medical evidence of the illness. People with IAD often misinterpret normal bodily sensations as signs of a serious medical condition and may spend a lot of time and energy seeking reassurance and medical attention.

The symptoms of IAD can vary in severity and can cause significant distress and impairment in daily life. Common symptoms include:

Frequent checking of the body for signs of illness

Excessive worry about health and illness

Fear of having a serious medical condition, such as cancer or heart disease

Misinterpretation of bodily sensations as signs of illness

Avoidance of medical appointments or tests due to fear of receiving bad news

Seeking multiple medical opinions and reassurance from doctors

Difficulty functioning in daily life due to health concerns

IAD can be diagnosed by a mental health professional, such as a psychiatrist or psychologist, who will evaluate the individual's symptoms and medical history.

Facts about illness anxiety disorder

Here are some facts about illness anxiety disorder (IAD):

IAD was previously known as hypochondriasis, but the term was changed in the latest edition of the Diagnostic and Statistical Manual of Mental Disorders (DSM-5) to better reflect the condition.

People with IAD often have a heightened awareness of bodily sensations and may misinterpret them as signs of a serious illness, even when there is no medical evidence to support this.

IAD affects approximately 1-5% of the general population, and is more common in women than men.

IAD can have a significant impact on an individual's daily life, causing distress and impairment in functioning, as well as excessive healthcare utilization and associated costs.

IAD is a distinct mental health condition and is not the same as malingering or factitious disorder, which involve intentional fabrication of symptoms for personal gain.

Cognitive-behavioral therapy (CBT) is the most commonly used treatment for IAD, and can be effective in reducing symptoms of anxiety and excessive health worries.

Other treatments for IAD may include exposure therapy, medication, and support groups.

IAD can co-occur with other mental health conditions, such as depression, anxiety disorders, and obsessive-compulsive disorder (OCD).

The exact causes of IAD are not fully understood, but genetic, environmental, and psychological factors may all play a role.

With proper diagnosis and treatment, individuals with IAD can learn to manage their symptoms and improve their quality of life.

Treatment for illness anxiety disorder

The treatment for illness anxiety disorder (IAD) typically involves psychotherapy, medication, or a combination of both. Here are some common treatments for IAD:

Cognitive-behavioral therapy (CBT): CBT is a type of psychotherapy that focuses on identifying and challenging negative thoughts and beliefs that contribute to excessive health anxiety. This therapy can help individuals develop coping strategies to manage their worries and avoid excessive checking and reassurance-seeking behaviors.

Exposure therapy: Exposure therapy is a type of CBT that involves gradually exposing individuals to their fears and anxieties in a controlled setting. This therapy can help individuals confront and overcome their health-related fears and reduce their overall anxiety.

Medication: Antidepressants, particularly selective serotonin reuptake inhibitors (SSRIs), are commonly used to treat IAD, as they can help reduce symptoms of anxiety and depression. Other medications, such as antipsychotics or anxiolytics, may be used in certain cases.

Mindfulness-based therapies: Mindfulness-based therapies, such as mindfulness-based stress reduction (MBSR) or acceptance and commitment therapy (ACT), may also be helpful in reducing anxiety and improving quality of life in individuals with IAD.

Support groups: Joining a support group or participating in group therapy can help individuals with IAD feel less alone and more understood. It can also provide an opportunity to learn from others and share coping strategies.

It's important to note that treatment for IAD should be individualized and based on the person's specific needs and preferences. Seeking professional help from a mental health provider is the first step in getting effective treatment for IAD.

Mysophobia is an extreme fear or phobia of germs or dirt. People with mysophobia have an irrational fear of contamination and may take extreme measures to avoid contact with germs, such as excessive hand washing or avoiding public places. Mysophobia is also known as germaphobia, bacillophobia, or bacteriophobia.

Mysophobia can be a debilitating condition that can interfere with daily life. It can cause anxiety, panic attacks, and obsessive-compulsive behaviors, such as constantly cleaning or sanitizing objects and surfaces. Mysophobia can also lead to social isolation, as people with this phobia may avoid social situations or interacting with others for fear of contamination.

Treatment for mysophobia typically involves cognitive-behavioral therapy (CBT), which aims to help people with phobias to gradually confront their fears and develop coping strategies to manage their anxiety. In some cases, medication may also be prescribed to help manage symptoms. If you or someone you know is struggling with mysophobia, it's important to seek help from a mental health professional.

Factors responsible for mysophobia

Mysophobia can be caused by a variety of factors, including:

Traumatic experiences: People who have had a traumatic experience related to contamination, such as getting sick after touching something dirty, may develop mysophobia as a way of protecting themselves from further harm.

Obsessive-compulsive disorder (OCD): Mysophobia can be a symptom of OCD, a condition characterized by intrusive and unwanted thoughts and repetitive behaviors.

Environmental factors: People who grew up in environments that emphasized cleanliness and hygiene, such as overly clean households, may be more likely to develop mysophobia.

Genetics: Mysophobia can sometimes run in families, suggesting that there may be a genetic component to the condition.

Anxiety and stress: People who are prone to anxiety and stress may be more likely to develop mysophobia as a way of coping with their feelings of fear and uncertainty.

It's important to note that the development of mysophobia is likely to be influenced by a combination of these factors, rather than any single cause.

Help for people suffering mysophobia

If you or someone you know is suffering from mysophobia, there are several ways to seek help:

Seek professional help: A mental health professional, such as a therapist or psychiatrist, can help diagnose and treat mysophobia. They can provide therapy, such as cognitive-behavioral therapy (CBT), and may also recommend medications to manage symptoms.

Join a support group: Support groups can provide a safe and supportive environment for people with mysophobia to share their experiences and learn from others.

Learn relaxation techniques: Relaxation techniques, such as deep breathing, meditation, and yoga, can help manage anxiety and stress associated with mysophobia.

Practice exposure therapy: Exposure therapy involves gradually exposing yourself to the things you fear, such as germs or dirty surfaces, in a safe and controlled way. This can help desensitize you to your fears over time.

Make lifestyle changes: Practicing good hygiene, such as washing your hands regularly and avoiding contact with sick people, can help reduce the risk of illness and may help ease fears of contamination.

Remember that seeking help for mysophobia is an important step in managing the condition and improving your quality of life. With the right treatment and support, it is possible to overcome this phobia and regain control of your life.

CHAPTER SEVEN: TIMELY HANDLING OF ACROPHOBIA

Acrophobia is a type of anxiety disorder that involves an irrational and persistent fear of heights or situations that involve heights, such as standing on a tall building or climbing a ladder. People with acrophobia may experience symptoms such as sweating, trembling, dizziness, and panic attacks when they are exposed to heights or even think about them.

Acrophobia can develop as a result of a traumatic experience related to heights, such as falling from a high place or witnessing someone else fall. It can also be a learned response, where a person has learned to associate heights with danger or discomfort. Other factors that may contribute to the development of acrophobia include genetics, brain chemistry, and certain life experiences.

Treatment for acrophobia may involve cognitive-behavioral therapy, which helps individuals to challenge and change their negative thoughts and beliefs about heights, as well as gradually expose them to heights in a safe and controlled manner. Medications such as anti-anxiety drugs may also be used to help manage the symptoms of acrophobia.

Places to be avoided by people suffering from acrophobia

People with acrophobia may want to avoid places that involve heights or have features that trigger their fear of heights. Some examples of places to be avoided may include:

Skyscrapers or tall buildings with open balconies or observation decks

Bridges, especially those that are suspension or see-through, like the glass-bottomed bridge in Zhangjiajie, China

Rooftops or high rooftops, such as those found in urban areas

Ferris wheels or other amusement park rides that elevate you to high heights

Ski lifts or gondolas that travel high above the ground or mountains

High cliffs, mountains, or hiking trails that require scaling heights or traversing ledges with steep drop-offs

Any activity that involves heights, such as bungee jumping, skydiving, or paragliding

It's important to note that avoiding these places may help to reduce anxiety, but it's also important to seek treatment for acrophobia to overcome the fear and improve quality of life.

Timely Treatment for acrophobia

There are several effective treatments for acrophobia, including:

Cognitive-behavioral therapy (CBT): This type of therapy focuses on changing negative thought patterns and behaviors associated with acrophobia. CBT may involve gradual exposure to heights in a controlled setting, which helps individuals to confront their fears and learn how to manage their anxiety.

Virtual reality exposure therapy (VRET): VRET is a form of exposure therapy that uses virtual reality technology to simulate heights and other anxiety-provoking situations. This type of therapy allows individuals to experience a safe and controlled environment while gradually facing their fears.

Medication: Certain medications, such as anti-anxiety drugs and beta-blockers, can be helpful in managing the symptoms of acrophobia. These medications can reduce feelings of anxiety and physical symptoms like rapid heart rate and sweating.

Relaxation techniques: Learning relaxation techniques, such as deep breathing

and progressive muscle relaxation, can help individuals to manage their anxiety

and reduce the physical symptoms associated with acrophobia.

Hypnotherapy: This type of therapy involves the use of hypnosis to help

individuals access their subconscious mind and change negative thought patterns

associated with acrophobia.

It's important to work with a mental health professional to determine the best

treatment approach for acrophobia. With proper treatment, many people with

acrophobia can learn to manage their fears and live a more fulfilling life.

CHAPTER EIGHT: OVERCOMING AEROPHOBIA

Aerophobia, also known as the fear of flying, is a common anxiety disorder that

affects a significant number of people worldwide. People with aerophobia may

experience symptoms such as panic attacks, rapid heartbeat, sweating, and difficulty breathing when they are faced with the prospect of flying or when they are on a plane.

Aerophobia can be caused by a variety of factors, including a traumatic experience during a flight, a fear of heights, claustrophobia, or a general anxiety disorder. Treatment options for aerophobia may include cognitive-behavioral therapy, exposure therapy, and medication.

Myths and facts about aerophobia

There are several myths about aerophobia, also known as the fear of flying, that are not supported by scientific evidence. Here are a few examples:

Myth: Flying is the most dangerous mode of transportation.

Fact: Flying is actually one of the safest modes of transportation. According to the National Safety Council, you are more likely to be killed by lightning, drowning, or a car accident than by an aviation accident.

Myth: Turbulence can cause a plane to crash.

Fact: Turbulence is a common occurrence during flights, but it rarely causes planes to crash. Modern planes are designed to withstand even severe turbulence, and pilots are trained to navigate through it safely.

Myth: Fear of flying is just a weakness.

Fact: Fear of flying is a real anxiety disorder that can be caused by a variety of factors, including a traumatic experience during a flight, a fear of heights, claustrophobia, or a general anxiety disorder. It is not a sign of weakness, and people with aerophobia should not feel ashamed or embarrassed about seeking help.

Myth: Drinking alcohol can help calm nerves during a flight.

Fact: Drinking alcohol can actually make aerophobia worse. Alcohol is a depressant that can increase anxiety and impair judgment, making it more difficult to cope with fear during a flight.

Myth: Medication is the only way to treat aerophobia.

Fact: While medication can be helpful for some people with aerophobia, it is not the only treatment option. Cognitive-behavioral therapy and exposure therapy have been shown to be effective in reducing fear of flying, and many people are able to overcome their fear without medication.

Treatment for people suffering aerophobia

There are several treatments available for people suffering from aerophobia, also known as the fear of flying. The most typical therapies are as follows:

Cognitive-behavioral therapy (CBT): This type of therapy is designed to help individuals identify and change negative thoughts and behaviors associated with flying. A mental health professional may use techniques such as exposure therapy, where the individual is gradually exposed to flying situations in a controlled environment, and cognitive restructuring, where negative thoughts are challenged and replaced with positive ones.

Medications: Anti-anxiety medications or sedatives may be prescribed by a healthcare provider to help manage symptoms of anxiety or panic during a flight. It is important to note that medications should only be taken under the supervision of a healthcare provider.

Relaxation techniques: Techniques such as deep breathing, meditation, and muscle relaxation can help individuals manage feelings of anxiety and promote relaxation during a flight.

Support groups: Joining a support group for individuals with aerophobia can be helpful for individuals to share their experiences and learn from others.

Virtual reality therapy: This type of therapy uses virtual reality technology to simulate flying experiences and help individuals desensitize to the fear of flying.

It is important to work with a mental health professional to determine the most effective treatment plan for an individual's specific needs. With the right treatment and support, many individuals are able to overcome their fear of flying and enjoy air travel.

CHAPTER NINE: PRACTICALLY DEALING WITH ASTRAPHOBIA

Astraphobia is the excessive and irrational fear of thunder and lightning. People with this phobia may experience intense anxiety, panic attacks, and avoidance behaviors when they are exposed to thunderstorms.

The fear of thunder and lightning is relatively common, but it becomes a phobia when it significantly interferes with a person's daily life. Astraphobia can develop due to a traumatic experience related to thunderstorms or lightning, or it can be a learned behavior from a family member or friend who also has the phobia.

History about Astraphobia

Astraphobia, also known as brontophobia, is affecting people of all ages and backgrounds. The origins of astraphobia can be traced back to ancient times when thunder and lightning were seen as manifestations of the gods and were often associated with divine punishment.

In many cultures, thunder and lightning were considered powerful and dangerous forces that had to be appeased or avoided. For example, in ancient Greece, thunderbolts were the weapon of Zeus, the king of the gods, and were seen as a symbol of his power and wrath. In Norse mythology, Thor, the god of thunder, was feared and revered for his ability to control lightning and thunder.

As scientific knowledge about weather patterns and atmospheric phenomena advanced, the fear of thunder and lightning became less associated with religious or supernatural beliefs and more recognized as a legitimate phobia.

How to overcome astraphobia

Overcoming astraphobia can be a gradual process, but with the right techniques and support, it is possible to manage and overcome the fear of thunder and lightning. Here are some ways to help manage astraphobia:

Seek Professional Help: A mental health professional can help identify the root cause of your astraphobia and develop a treatment plan to help you manage your fear. This may include exposure therapy, cognitive-behavioral therapy, or medication.

Practice Relaxation Techniques: Deep breathing, progressive muscle relaxation, and visualization can help you manage anxiety during a thunderstorm. These techniques can help you relax and feel more in control.

Create a Safe Space: Creating a comfortable and safe environment during a thunderstorm can help reduce anxiety. This may include playing soothing music, using noise-cancelling headphones and other related devices.

Trypanophobia is the extreme fear or phobia of needles or injections. It is a common phobia that affects many people, and it can cause significant distress and avoidance behavior in individuals who experience it.

The fear of needles can develop due to various reasons, including traumatic experiences during childhood, fear of pain or discomfort, anxiety about the medical procedures, or simply due to a general fear of the unknown.

Factors responsible for trypanophobia

There are several factors that can contribute to the development of trypanophobia, including:

Past traumatic experiences: A previous negative experience with needles, such as a painful or traumatic injection, can cause an individual to develop a fear of needles.

Anxiety or phobia disorder: People who are prone to anxiety or phobia disorders may be more likely to develop trypanophobia.

Genetics: Research has shown that there may be a genetic component to the development of phobias, including trypanophobia.

Parental influence: Children who have parents with a fear of needles are more likely to develop the same phobia.

Cultural factors: Different cultures have different attitudes towards needles and injections. Some cultures may view needles as a source of danger or harm, which can contribute to the development of a phobia.

Lack of information: Individuals who do not understand the purpose of medical procedures involving needles, or who have not been adequately informed about the process, may be more likely to develop a fear of needles.

It is important to note that trypanophobia can be a complex condition, and the factors that contribute to its development can vary widely between individuals. A healthcare professional can help to identify the specific factors that may be contributing to an individual's phobia and develop a treatment plan accordingly.

Symptoms of trypanophobia can include sweating, rapid heartbeat, dizziness, nausea, fainting, panic attacks, and avoidance behavior.

Treatment options for trypanophobia can include cognitive-behavioral therapy (CBT), exposure therapy, relaxation techniques, and medication. CBT can help individuals to identify and challenge their negative thoughts and beliefs about needles and injections. Exposure therapy involves gradually exposing the individual to needles or injections in a controlled and safe environment to help them overcome their fear.

In some cases, medications such as beta-blockers or sedatives may also be prescribed to help manage the physical symptoms of anxiety during medical procedures involving needles. It is essential to talk to a healthcare professional about treatment options if you or someone you know is experiencing trypanophobia.

Xenophobia is the fear or hatred of foreigners, people from different cultures, or people who are perceived to be different from oneself. This can manifest as prejudice, discrimination, or aggression towards individuals or groups who are seen as outsiders. Xenophobia can be based on a variety of factors, such as race, ethnicity, nationality, religion, language, or socio-economic status.

Xenophobia can have serious social, economic, and political consequences. It can lead to social exclusion, discrimination, and violence against individuals and groups who are seen as different. It can also create barriers to trade and international cooperation, and can undermine efforts to promote diversity, tolerance, and understanding.

Historical effects of Xenophobia

Here are some historical effects of xenophobia:

Colonialism: Xenophobia played a significant role in the age of colonialism, as European powers used it to justify their conquest and exploitation of non-European peoples. Europeans portrayed non-Europeans as inferior and uncivilized, justifying their colonialism as a "civilizing mission."

Genocide: Xenophobia has led to numerous genocides throughout history. For example, the Holocaust in Nazi Germany was fueled by anti-Semitic sentiment, while the Rwandan genocide was driven by anti-Tutsi sentiment.

Immigration policies: Xenophobia has influenced immigration policies throughout history, with many countries implementing discriminatory policies that limit the entry of immigrants based on their race, ethnicity, religion, or nationality. For example, the United States had exclusionary laws targeting Chinese immigrants in the late 1800s and early 1900s.

Racism: Xenophobia is often intertwined with racism, with people of different races being targeted for discrimination and violence. For example, the Jim Crow laws in the United States enforced racial segregation and discrimination against African Americans, while apartheid in South Africa enforced a system of racial segregation and discrimination against black people.

Global conflicts: Xenophobia has contributed to many global conflicts throughout history, with people of different nationalities or ethnicities being pitted against each other. For example, World War I and World War II were fueled by nationalism and xenophobia, with different nations seeing themselves as superior to others.

Overall, xenophobia has had a significant impact on history, leading to discrimination, violence, and conflict. It continues to be a pressing issue today, with many people and nations still grappling with issues related to immigration, racism, and discrimination.

Root causes of xenophobia

Xenophobia is a complex social and psychological phenomenon that can have multiple root causes. Some of the common factors that contribute to xenophobia include:

Fear of the unknown: People often fear what they do not understand, and this fear can manifest as xenophobia when applied to people from different cultures or backgrounds.

Economic insecurity: Economic insecurity, such as job loss or financial instability, can create a sense of competition and resentment towards people who are seen as outsiders. This can lead to blaming immigrants or foreign workers for taking jobs or resources from locals.

Historical and cultural factors: Historical conflicts, cultural differences, and past trauma can create deep-seated resentment and prejudice towards certain groups of people.

Political rhetoric and media influence: Political leaders and media outlets can contribute to xenophobia by promoting a narrative that portrays certain groups of people as threats to national security, culture, or identity.

Lack of exposure and education: Lack of exposure to people from different cultures or limited access to education about diversity and inclusion can reinforce stereotypes and biases.

It is important to recognize that xenophobia is a complex phenomenon that can have multiple causes. Addressing these root causes requires a multifaceted approach that involves education, social policies, and a commitment to promoting diversity and inclusion.

How to combat xenophobia

Combatting xenophobia requires a concerted effort at multiple levels, including individuals, communities, and governments. Here are some ways to combat xenophobia:

Education and awareness: Education and awareness-raising activities can help combat xenophobia by promoting understanding and empathy for people from different backgrounds. This can involve school programs, community events, and media campaigns that promote diversity, inclusion, and multiculturalism.

Interpersonal engagement: Encouraging personal interaction between people from different backgrounds can help break down stereotypes and prejudices. This can involve community building activities, volunteering, and engaging in cross-cultural dialogue.

Advocacy and policy: Advocacy and policy initiatives can help combat xenophobia by promoting laws and policies that protect the rights and dignity of immigrants and refugees, combat discrimination, and promote inclusion. This can involve advocacy efforts, lobbying, and supporting civil society organizations.

Media responsibility: Media outlets should be responsible in their reporting and avoid sensationalizing stories that could feed into xenophobic attitudes. They should also promote diversity and positive representations of people from different backgrounds.

Personal responsibility: Individuals can combat xenophobia by examining their own attitudes and biases, challenging stereotypes, and promoting empathy and understanding. They can also speak out against xenophobic attitudes and behaviors in their communities.

Overall, combatting xenophobia requires a sustained effort from all levels of society. By promoting education, awareness, and policy initiatives, we can create a more inclusive and welcoming society for all people.

CHAPTER TWELVE: HIDDEN FACTORS ABOUT DEATH PHOBIA

Death phobia, also known as thanatophobia or death anxiety, is a persistent fear of death or dying. This fear can cause significant distress and interfere with a person's daily life. While some level of fear of death is normal, death phobia is characterized by an excessive and irrational fear that can lead to avoidance of anything related to death or dying.

Some common symptoms of death phobia may include:

Constant thoughts or worries about death

Avoiding situations or activities that may increase the risk of death

Physical symptoms such as trembling, sweating, or rapid heartbeat when thinking about death

Panic attacks related to death

Difficulty sleeping due to fears about death

Factors that cause death phobia

There are several factors that can contribute to the development of death phobia or thanatophobia. These may include:

Personal beliefs and attitudes: A person's personal beliefs and attitudes about death and dying can play a significant role in the development of death phobia. For example, a person who believes that death is a punishment or a final end may be more likely to develop a fear of death.

Traumatic experiences: Traumatic experiences such as the sudden death of a loved one or witnessing a traumatic event can contribute to the development of death phobia.

Cultural or societal influences: Cultural or societal attitudes and beliefs about death and dying can also contribute to the development of death phobia. In some cultures, death is seen as a natural part of life, while in others it is seen as a taboo or something to be feared.

Anxiety and other mental health conditions: People who have anxiety or other mental health conditions may be more likely to develop death phobia.

Age: Death phobia is more common in older adults, as they may be more aware of their own mortality and have experienced the loss of loved ones.

It is important to note that death phobia is a treatable condition, and seeking professional help can be beneficial in managing the symptoms of the condition.

Treatment for death phobia

Treatment for death phobia or thanatophobia typically involves a combination of therapy and medication, depending on the severity of the condition and the individual's specific needs. Some common treatment options include:

Cognitive-behavioral therapy (CBT): CBT is a type of therapy that focuses on identifying and changing negative thoughts and behaviors. In the case of death phobia, CBT may involve challenging negative thoughts and beliefs about death and developing coping strategies to manage anxiety and fear.

Exposure therapy: Exposure therapy involves gradually exposing the individual to situations or objects related to death in a safe and controlled environment. This can help to desensitize the person to their fears and reduce anxiety over time.

Medication: Medications such as anti-anxiety or antidepressant medications may be prescribed to help manage the symptoms of death phobia.

Support groups: Joining a support group of individuals who are also struggling with death phobia can be helpful in providing a sense of community and reducing feelings of isolation.

Mindfulness techniques: Mindfulness techniques such as meditation, deep breathing, and yoga can be helpful in managing anxiety and promoting relaxation.

It is important to note that seeking professional help from a mental health provider is the best way to receive an accurate diagnosis and appropriate treatment plan for death phobia.

Animal phobia, also known as zoophobia, is a type of anxiety disorder characterized by an intense and irrational fear of animals. This fear can be triggered by any type of animal, including dogs, cats, snakes, spiders, birds, or insects, and can range from mild discomfort to a debilitating panic attack. Brief description of these animal phobias are :

Dog phobia

Dog phobia, also known as cynophobia, is a type of animal phobia characterized by an irrational and intense fear of dogs. People with dog phobia may experience a range of physical and psychological symptoms when confronted with dogs or even just the thought of them.

Some common symptoms of dog phobia include:

Feelings of extreme anxiety, panic, or terror when in the presence of dogs or even thinking about them.

Avoiding places where dogs might be present, such as parks or neighborhoods known for dog ownership.

Difficulty breathing, trembling, sweating, or feeling nauseous when encountering dogs.

Experiencing intense and persistent thoughts about the possibility of encountering dogs, even in situations where they are unlikely to be present.

Dog phobia can be treated through various forms of therapy, including cognitive-behavioral therapy (CBT) and exposure therapy. In CBT, a therapist will work with the patient to identify the underlying thoughts and beliefs that are contributing to their fear and teach them new coping skills. Exposure therapy involves gradually exposing the patient to dogs, starting with mild exposure and gradually increasing the intensity until the patient learns to manage their fear more effectively. In some cases, medications such as beta-blockers or anti-anxiety drugs may also be prescribed to help manage symptoms.

Cat phobia

Cat phobia, also known as ailurophobia, is a type of animal phobia characterized by an irrational and intense fear of cats. People with cat phobia may experience a range of physical and psychological symptoms when confronted with cats or even just the thought of them.

Some common symptoms of cat phobia include:

Feelings of extreme anxiety, panic, or terror when in the presence of cats or even thinking about them.

Avoiding places where cats might be present, such as homes of friends or family who own cats or neighborhoods known for cat ownership.

Difficulty breathing, trembling, sweating, or feeling nauseous when encountering cats.

Experiencing intense and persistent thoughts about the possibility of encountering cats, even in situations where they are unlikely to be present.

Cat phobia can be treated through various forms of therapy, including cognitive-behavioral therapy (CBT) and exposure therapy. In CBT, a therapist will work with the patient to identify the underlying thoughts and beliefs that are contributing to their fear and teach them new coping skills. Exposure therapy involves gradually exposing the patient to cats, starting with mild exposure and gradually increasing the intensity until the patient learns to manage their fear more effectively. In some cases, medications such as beta-blockers or anti-anxiety drugs may also be prescribed to help manage symptoms.

Snake phobia

Snake phobia, also known as ophidiophobia, is a type of animal phobia characterized by an irrational and intense fear of snakes. People with snake phobia may experience a range of physical and psychological symptoms when confronted with snakes or even just the thought of them.

Some common symptoms of snake phobia include:

Feelings of extreme anxiety, panic, or terror when in the presence of snakes or even thinking about them.

Avoiding places where snakes might be present, such as parks or nature reserves known for snake sightings.

Difficulty breathing, trembling, sweating, or feeling nauseous when encountering snakes.

Experiencing intense and persistent thoughts about the possibility of encountering snakes, even in situations where they are unlikely to be present.

Snake phobia can be treated through various forms of therapy, including cognitive-behavioral therapy (CBT) and exposure therapy. In CBT, a therapist will work with the patient to identify the underlying thoughts and beliefs that are contributing to their fear and teach them new coping skills. Exposure therapy involves gradually exposing the patient to snakes, starting with mild exposure and gradually increasing the intensity until the patient learns to manage their fear more effectively. In some cases, medications such as beta-blockers or anti-anxiety drugs may also be prescribed to help manage symptoms.

Spider phobia

Spider phobia, also known as arachnophobia, is a type of animal phobia characterized by an irrational and intense fear of spiders. People with spider phobia may experience a range of physical and psychological symptoms when confronted with spiders or even just the thought of them.

Some common symptoms of spider phobia include:

Feelings of extreme anxiety, panic, or terror when in the presence of spiders or even thinking about them.

Avoiding places where spiders might be present, such as basements, attics, or outdoor areas with lots of vegetation.

Difficulty breathing, trembling, sweating, or feeling nauseous when encountering spiders.

Experiencing intense and persistent thoughts about the possibility of encountering spiders, even in situations where they are unlikely to be present.

Spider phobia can be treated through various forms of therapy, including cognitive-behavioral therapy (CBT) and exposure therapy. In CBT, a therapist will work with the patient to identify the underlying thoughts and beliefs that are contributing to their fear and teach them new coping skills. Exposure therapy involves gradually exposing the patient to spiders, starting with mild exposure and gradually increasing the intensity until the patient learns to manage their fear more effectively. In some cases, medications such as beta-blockers or anti-anxiety drugs may also be prescribed to help manage symptoms.

Bird phobia

Bird phobia, also known as ornithophobia, is a type of animal phobia characterized by an irrational and intense fear of birds. People with bird phobia may experience a range of physical and psychological symptoms when confronted with birds or even just the thought of them.

Some common symptoms of bird phobia include:

Feelings of extreme anxiety, panic, or terror when in the presence of birds or even thinking about them.

Avoiding places where birds might be present, such as parks or outdoor areas with lots of bird activity.

Difficulty breathing, trembling, sweating, or feeling nauseous when encountering birds.

Experiencing intense and persistent thoughts about the possibility of encountering birds, even in situations where they are unlikely to be present.

Bird phobia can be treated through various forms of therapy, including cognitive-behavioral therapy (CBT) and exposure therapy. In CBT, a therapist will work with the patient to identify the underlying thoughts and beliefs that are contributing to their fear and teach them new coping skills. Exposure therapy involves gradually exposing the patient to birds, starting with mild exposure and gradually increasing the intensity until the patient learns to manage their fear more effectively. In some cases, medications such as beta-blockers or anti-anxiety drugs may also be prescribed to help manage symptoms.

Insect phobia

Insect phobia, also known as entomophobia, is a type of animal phobia characterized by an irrational and intense fear of insects. People with insect phobia may experience a range of physical and psychological symptoms when confronted with insects or even just the thought of them.

Some common symptoms of insect phobia include:

Feelings of extreme anxiety, panic, or terror when in the presence of insects or even thinking about them.

Avoiding places where insects might be present, such as outdoor areas with lots of vegetation or indoor spaces where insects are common, such as basements or attics.

Difficulty breathing, trembling, sweating, or feeling nauseous when encountering insects.

Experiencing intense and persistent thoughts about the possibility of encountering insects, even in situations where they are unlikely to be present.

Insect phobia can be treated through various forms of therapy, including cognitive-behavioral therapy (CBT) and exposure therapy. In CBT, a therapist will work with the patient to identify the underlying thoughts and beliefs that are contributing to their fear and teach them new coping skills. Exposure therapy involves gradually exposing the patient to insects, starting with mild exposure and gradually increasing the intensity until the patient learns to manage their fear more effectively. In some cases, medications such as beta-blockers or anti-anxiety drugs may also be prescribed to help manage symptoms.

Some common symptoms of animal phobia include:

Feeling an overwhelming sense of fear or panic when in the presence of animals or even thinking about them.

Avoiding places where animals might be present, such as parks or pet stores.

Difficulty breathing, trembling, sweating, or feeling nauseous when encountering animals.

Experiencing intense and persistent thoughts about the possibility of encountering animals, even in situations where they are unlikely to be present.

Animal phobia can be treated through various forms of therapy, including cognitive-behavioral therapy (CBT) and exposure therapy. In CBT, a therapist will work with the patient to identify the underlying thoughts and beliefs that are contributing to their fear and teach them new coping skills. Exposure therapy involves gradually exposing the patient to the source of their fear, starting with mild exposure and gradually increasing the intensity until the patient learns to manage their fear more effectively. In some cases, medications such as beta-blockers or anti-anxiety drugs may also be prescribed to help manage symptoms.

CONCLUSION

Since we live in a world full of unexpected events, it is obvious that phobias are as old as mankind and will always exist. No matter how self-assured you are, you will eventually develop phobias. You might feel the most helpless or afraid individual on Earth when that happens. It's interesting to note that if you can understand and manage your phobia, you won't have much to fret about. Furthermore, understanding various phobias is a benefit because it enables one to take a variety of useful remedial measures.

www.ingramcontent.com/pod-product-compliance
Lightning Source LLC
Chambersburg PA
CBHW081559270726
48657CB00029B/3380